Copyright © 2023 by Feliz Corral

All rights reserved. No part of this book may be reproduced in any manner whatsoever without written permission except in the case of brief quotations embodied in critical articles and reviews.

First Printing, 2023

GRANDMA'S LITTLE HELPER

FELIZ CORRAL

GRANDMA'S LITTLE HELPER

Dedication

To my mother, Judith.

Thank you for being my mom and my best friend. Thank you for everything that you sacrificed for me and my brother. Thank you for being the lovely grandma that you are to my Lily. Thank you for all the love that you always have for my husband.

I love you and miss you all the time,

E.L.M

One day grandma came to visit...

Every time I see Grandma, she looks so beautiful and full of life. She kisses and tickles me. I'm always so happy when she comes to see me.

She is always looking for her glasses, so I help her find them.

I love them because they scratch the back of my mouth so well.

She always needs help falling asleep. If she doesn't grab me, sit in the rocking chair, and sing me a song, she will not fall asleep.

When she's about to leave, she looks sad. I guess she misses me very much when I'm not with her. But, before she leaves, she always kisses me allover and tells me:

-What would I have done if you weren't here?
Grandma loves you
forever more.

ABOUT THE AUTHOR

She was born in the year 1993 in the Dominican Republic. Her parents worked hard to give her the best education that was available. After graduating from high school, she entered Law school at Pontificia Universidad Católica Madre y Maestra, graduating in 2015. Soon after, she married her childhood friend and forever partner in 2017. She started to study psychology at TROY University Online. After traveling the world in 2021, they welcomed their first baby. Now stationed in the Armed Forces Pacific, Japan, she continues to portray her life experience through her writing.

Printed in the USA
CPSIA information can be obtained
at www.ICGtesting.com
LVHW070304141023
760911LV00014B/203